GW01017964

wireless computing

flexible business communications
for organisations of all sizes

consultant editor:	Marc Beishon
sub-editor:	Lesley Malachowski
production manager:	Lisa Robertson
design:	Halo Design
commercial director:	Ed Hicks
publishing director:	Tom Nash
chief operating officer:	Andrew Main Wilson
chairman:	George Cox

Published for the Institute of Directors and Toshiba
by Director Publications Ltd
116 Pall Mall London SW1Y 5ED
T 020 7766 8910 W www.iod.com

© Copyright July 2004 Director Publications Ltd
A CIP record for this book is available from the British Library
Printed and bound in Great Britain.

Toshiba Computer Systems Division

Toshiba Computer Systems Division (CSD) is a wholly owned UK subsidiary of the multinational Toshiba Corporation, a global leader in a wide range of technologically advanced products. Toshiba CSD is a specialist in wireless and mobile computing, with responsibility for sales of notebook computers, pocket PCs and associated options, peripherals and services.

Best In Class

As a worldwide market leader in both the business and home markets, Toshiba CSD prides itself on being consistently best-in-class when it comes to mobile and wireless computing. Since introducing the world's first notebook computer in 1985, Toshiba has continued to lead the development and innovation of technology in the mobile and wireless computing world.

Toshiba is focused on mobility and develops technologies that can deliver the digital wireless office. Coupled with efficient and reliable service capabilities through local and global alliances, Toshiba produces market-leading mobility products that enable wireless working in the office, on the move and at home.

Wireless & Mobility

Toshiba CSD's expertise in mobility and wireless computing products is a result of its research and development, which is concentrated on ensuring that the needs of mobile computing users are satisfied. As a result, Toshiba has focussed its business on creating world-class wireless computing solutions for today's increasingly mobile business and home communities.

Toshiba's focus is on innovations in wireless computing products, peripherals and services, partnerships, clear customer focus and concentration on its core strengths in miniaturisation and mobility.

Toshiba offers the customer an unrivalled combination of technology, experience and the skills needed to turn the vision of 'always-on wireless computing' into a reality.

W www.computers.toshiba.co.uk T 0870 444 8944

CONTENTS

Marc Beishon, Bryan Betts, Nick Langley, Malcolm Wheatley and Sally Whittle
are independent business and technology writers.

Get to work in under a minute.

**MOBILE
TECHNOLOGY**

Why waste time commuting when Toshiba's wireless solutions le
you start your working day in a more relaxed fashion? The Tecra M:
is powered by Intel® Centrino™ Mobile Technology for cutting-edg
wireless performance and seamless connectivity via integrate
Wireless LAN*. It's all you need to get ahead on work from you
kitchen table – while enjoying a leisurely breakfast.

Choose freedom.
www.toshiba.co.uk/computers or telephone 0870 444 8933.

shiba recommends Microsoft® Windows® XP Professional for Mobile Computing

TOSHIBA

TOSHIBA

the new world of wireless

**George Cox, Director General
Institute of Directors**

In a few years' time, the idea of ever having been tethered by wires to a fixed communications infrastructure will seem remarkably quaint. Devices such as laptop and palmtop computers are already displacing conventional desktop computers. Use of wireless communications to link these devices to the Internet and corporate private networks is growing dramatically. Wireless LANs (WLANs) at 'hotspots' on company sites and in public areas such as airports, hotels, railway termini, motorway service areas and coffee shops are the most obvious manifestations. However, the growing use of the mobile telephone networks for Internet access via the General Packet Radio Service (GPRS) and increasingly the broadband 3G networks, is equally important. It is becoming practical to be 'always on' through WLANs in the home, driven from mass market broadband connections, WLANs as part of the corporate network in the office, plus hot spots, GPRS and 3G networks whilst on the move. For many organisations, the increased workforce flexibility enabled by wireless computing can drive down fixed costs whilst genuinely improving staff morale and job satisfaction.

This Director's Guide explores the scope for major improvements in both customer service and productivity flowing from wireless computing. Whether by having sales staff on the road that can place and confirm orders immediately through wireless linked laptop computers, or by cost reduction in inventory control systems using radio frequency identification chips (RFID) in wireless enabled warehouses, the opportunities are ours to exploit. On the shopfloor, in the office and in the boardroom there is the potential to transform business processes and gain competitive advantage. The key will be to blend these new technologies with new ways of working, training and motivating employees to grasp the opportunities.

As with any powerful new tool, wireless computing needs to be treated with respect. Implementation needs to be carefully planned and budgeted. Staff do need to be properly trained, both to exploit the benefits and to avoid security pitfalls, such as inadvertently sharing their files with all the other users in a WLAN hotspot! Wireless networks need carefully designed security systems and firewalls. Advice on best practice is widely available.

The IoD is exploiting these new opportunities, as regular users of the 'hotspot' in 123 Pall Mall can attest. This guide, produced in association with Toshiba – to whom we are most grateful for their support – can help you evaluate the benefits for your organisation.

Finally, please also visit www.iod.com/wirelesscomputing for all the latest news, information and advice on this key business topic.

implementation: the critical phase

Andy Bass, General Manager, Toshiba Computer Systems Division

The last two years have seen a dramatic leap in the adoption and implementation of wireless computing technology. You are unlikely to see a new notebook introduced into the market nowadays without some form of wireless connectivity, and the appearance of hotspot technologies in public places from coffee shops to train stations has put us one step closer to ubiquitous wireless computing.

The commercial realities of getting the right information to the right people, quickly and cost effectively means that wireless computing technology can make a significant contribution to the success of a business. By helping people to work more productively and efficiently, you can drive revenues, increase customer satisfaction and enhance competitive advantage.

We have now entered a critical phase in wireless computing. As a worldwide leader in wireless products, we are increasingly being asked by companies how to drive business benefits from mobile and wireless technologies, rather than just what technologies exist. Businesses have moved through initial adoption to reach implementation, and this stage is critical. Get implementation right and you could have a more efficient, more productive and happier workforce. Get it wrong and you face wasting investments, compromising network security and overworking employees.

At a time when budgets are tight and every investment counts, can companies really afford to be investing in technology without understanding its business benefits and why they are introducing it?

This guide is a comprehensive overview of the current thinking on wireless computing and will focus on how you and your company can realise the benefits of the technology. For example, we focus on the rise of flexible working, what wireless devices are available, hotspot technology, GPRS access and wireless security; we also examine how these issues affect productivity, ROI and competitive advantage.

We explain six steps to wireless computing, how to educate staff to get the best from wireless technology and how to optimise the cost of your wireless computing investment. Case studies throughout this guide demonstrate how business advantage can be achieved.

The next 12 months will be an important time for businesses implementing wireless computing. Stability, reducing risk, ensuring business continuity and a clear understanding of the benefits of this technology will be critical. This guide aims to demonstrate how wireless computing is relevant to your business and it also gives you the knowledge and information that will enable you to put it to the most effective use.

TOSHIBA

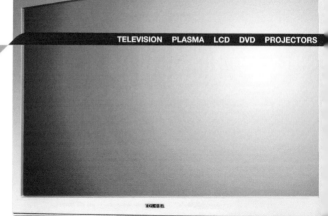

24Z33

ET1

RDXS32

PICTURE
FRAME **3**

36ZP48

23W146

DR3

www.toshiba.co.uk

Brochure Line: 08704 424 42

what wireless will mean to you

Malcolm Wheatley, business and technology writer, charts the rapid ascent of wireless computing and outlines the key issues affecting businesses

Despite what the computer industry often says, 'breakthrough' technologies don't happen very often. However, wireless computing (Wi-Fi or wireless fidelity, as it's sometimes called, and which we major on in this guide) – and also GPRS/3G mobile networks – look set to become one of those rare technologies, ranking alongside the fax machine, the notebook PC and mobile voice phone.

That's because wireless computing has a central set of features that can change and shape the way that companies and individuals go about their daily business. These include the ability to:

- send and receive information at high speed while on the move – in airports, hotels, service stations and even coffee shops and burger bars

- work in company premises to enable wireless connections for staff with handheld and laptop computers as they move around

- enable a wide spectrum of business applications that integrate with 'head office' to be used remotely – salesforce automation, field service engineering,

EXECUTIVE SUMMARY

- wireless computing has enjoyed possibly the fastest rollout ever seen in the computer industry

- wireless networks are cheaper to set up than hardwired cable networks and easier to upgrade and expand

- the use of wireless networks in the home is proving popular – particularly in Europe

- there are drawbacks, including outstanding issues concerning security and difficulty in calculating bottom-line benefits to financial services – any application where up-to-the-minute, sophisticated networking is needed

☐ effortlessly create a wireless environment in remote locations, including satellite offices and workers' homes

what's happening in the here and now?

And wireless computing is here now. It is not some pie in the sky technology. It has enjoyed probably the fastest rollout ever seen in the computer industry, with networking equipment, wireless-enabled laptop computers and roaming points in places such as railway stations, all coming together over the last year or so.

Indeed, wireless computing offers much the same 'disruptive' impact as the mobile phone. Yet again, the dimension of mobility is being added to a huge installed base of appliances that people use on a daily basis. Yet again, the appliances in question – computers – have both personal and business uses. And, yet again, they enable people to communicate with other people.

But although it's a potent mix, it's still unclear what sort of brew will eventually emerge. Partly, the problem is one of fragmentation: 'wireless' is not just one technology, but several – Wi-Fi and GPRS/3G mobile networks being the two key 'carriers'. The appliances, too, are fragmented: as well as laptop computers they include dedicated email appliances such as the BlackBerry as well as various forms of personal digital assistants (PDAs). And wireless computing is still well down the adoption curve. The 'early adopters' are on board, but the mainstream masses who will define how it is used are not.

rapid growth

What is clear is that wireless in all its forms is growing rapidly. According to InfoTech, a research company, expenditure on creating or enlarging wireless networks which use wireless technology to replace cable in office blocks, factories and, increasingly, homes, totalled $550m in 2002, and is estimated to reach $1.3bn in 2008. Separately, analyst group Gartner predicts that the number of users connected to wireless networks is expected to soar from 4.2m in 2003 to 31m in 2007.

WHAT IS WI-FI?

Wi-Fi is a technology that lets users surf the Internet and access office networks wirelessly – as long as they are within reach of an access point. The area covered by an access point is known as a 'hotspot'.

The characteristics of Wi-Fi are:

- [ ] it is high speed. The minimum specification is up to 11 megabits a second, which is the same as many 'hard wired' office computer networks

- [ ] it is based on standards. There is a family of standards that offers different speeds – four are presently available – for general and more specialist applications

- [ ] it carries computer information in the same way as normal office networks. This means wireless access to standard office applications, special in-house applications such as stock control and, of course, full access to the Internet

- [ ] it is only intended for short distance communications. Depending on the standard, distances vary from 60 to 300 feet – faster standards work over the shortest distances

A wireless network can also carry voice communications as well as computer data – opening up existing opportunities for new types of mobile phone. In addition to Wi-Fi, there are GPRS/3G networks that enable wireless access via mobile phone networks. Although access is widespread, speeds are slower than Wi-Fi.

the appeal of wireless

In the corporate world, the driver behind such growth is cost. Computers underpin the way that business works, whether it's through allowing people to communicate with each other via email, or through running the various back office 'enterprise' systems that process customer orders, manage inventory, maintain the purchase ledger, etc. But computers need connecting to other computers to carry out these tasks – and cabling buildings is expensive. Wireless networks don't need cables: radio waves carry the data traffic instead.

There are other advantages. Wireless networks are not only cheaper to install than cabling, but also cheaper and easier to upgrade and add new users to. They permit more flexible use of office space – desks can be anywhere, and can be moved at will – as cabling considerations become irrelevant. Personal productivity improves, too: laptop-bearing employees can receive and act on emails and other electronic communication wherever they are within the network – waiting for a meeting to start, in transit between offices, or at another corporate location altogether.

home use of wi-fi

Wireless networks are also becoming popular in the home. As in the corporate world, home-based workers appreciate the flexibility of being able to work wherever they want without installing expensive cabling. But corporate employees are also busily installing wireless networks in the home, especially when the home is connected to the Internet over broadband.

Over 80 per cent of Microsoft's UK employees have wireless networks at home, says Steve Harvey, director of people and culture at Microsoft UK. The company has a policy of promoting it, he says. "Not only does it let people experience the digital lifestyle, but it also helps them to become more effective from a work point of view," he explains.

And Harvey himself is one of the aforementioned 80 per cent. Instead of being isolated in the study as he catches up on work at home, "I can work alongside the family, in a way that is non-obtrusive to family life," he says.

As more and more computers come with Wi-Fi capability built in – often at no extra cost – home Wi-Fi use is booming. According to a report from analysts In-Stat/MDR, some 23 million Wi-Fi base units were sold worldwide in 2003, with most of them being connected to the Internet.

While many of these are in the US, the fastest growing geographic region for home Wi-Fi is Europe, where shipments have risen from nine per cent of total sales in 2002 to 15 per cent in 2003. In-Stat/MDR concludes that much of this was driven by the sharp growth in home broadband connections throughout 2003.

But in terms of media hype, it's Wi-Fi 'hotspots' that have captured the most attention. These are once again wireless networks with a small footprint, but are intended to allow public access to the Internet – and from the Internet, if desired, back to the corporate network.

The hotspot phenomenon grew out of the US, where Internet-minded individuals made them available at no cost, with connection availability spread by word of mouth and by 'war chalking', where users would chalk symbols on walls and pavements to indicate that access was possible at a particular location.

WHERE CAN YOU USE WI-FI?

We are focusing on wireless computing – or Wi-Fi – as we're calling it for short – in this guide. It can be deployed (and enjoyed) in a number of contexts, both for business and pleasure.

There are three main places where you can use Wi-Fi:

- [ ] in the office or on company premises. Not only can wireless networks replace costly and more inflexible fixed wire systems, they can make hitherto unwired parts of your company available for flexible access

- [ ] on the move. The most talked about application of Wi-Fi is in so-called 'hotspots', public places where users can get linked up to company networks and the Internet while away from the office. Also GPRS enables wireless access via mobile phone networks and wirelessly enabled notebooks

- [ ] in the home. Millions of enthusiasts worldwide are already running wireless Internet and home entertainment networks in their homes – and they can also be used for home working applications

Increasingly, however, hotspots on this side of the Atlantic have been installed in places that are either frequented by business travellers, or which would like to be more often frequented by business travellers. Hotels, airports and convention centres are examples of the former category, whereas restaurants and fast-food outlets are examples of the latter. The logic: while sipping your coffee, or waiting for a flight, why not catch-up on your email, or check out your favourite websites?

Thus far, hotels have proved to be the most popular location for hotspots, says Ian Fogg, an analyst with Jupiter Research. Some 44 per cent of Wi-Fi sessions that took place during 2003 did so in hotels – despite the ready availability of hotspots in other locations. A hotel room is a more comfortable and appropriately-equipped place to work, he suggests, with ready availability of power sockets, as well as privacy.

Of course, wireless computing is also possible away from both home, office and hotspot. The so-called GSM, GPRS and now third generation (3G) mobile telephony services are offering progressively faster data services for accessing applications and the Internet on the move, although even with the latest 3G, speeds are slower than Wi-Fi.

issues to consider

Nonetheless, there are drawbacks with any technology. With Wi-Fi, security is a major concern: few people understand how much of the information on their computers is potentially visible to others sharing a hotspot or wireless network.

Another factor is how to determine the business case for wireless investment. The direct cost of avoiding physical cable installation may be straightforward – but applications in and out the office will be hard to measure in terms of productivity and payback.

One message that's emerging is to think less in terms of counting every penny – and instead get on and experiment. Users' feedback on the undoubtable value that many will report can be used for wider rollouts, as and when appropriate.

the rise of flexible working

Marc Beishon, business and technology writer, charts the increasing take-up of flexible working practices and the advances in communications and computing technology that have enabled it

Which comes first – the desire to work more flexibly, or the enabling technology that allows such working to take place, so creating demand?

The answer is probably that the two go hand in hand, with wireless computing and mobile phones fuelling a desire for flexible working on the part of workers, and a drive for increased productivity through working closer to customers on the part of employers.

A measure of how far we've come in the move away from the traditional idea of the office comes from a study conducted for Intel by the Economist Intelligence Unit. The 'nine to five' routine is becoming a thing of the past for European and Middle Western business workers, the research, entitled Destination Wireless, finds. Among the key points are:

☐ more working time is being spent out of the office – currently respondents spend a third of the average working day outside a static work base, and predict that this proportion is set to grow to just under half in two years time

☐ working day patterns are becoming increasingly fragmented – driven in part by globalisation, professionals cited the need to work with colleagues in other countries/offices as part of a virtual team as a key driver in the changing nature of their work pattern

☐ more than a third of those questioned cited remote colleagues as their main day-to-day contacts, reflecting the increasing irrelevance of location

flexible trends

According to the *Complete Guide to Flexible Working*, from www.flexibility.co.uk and Toshiba, there are many types of technology-enabled trends in the flexible working arena. These include teleworking; 'fleeing the workplace in order to work' and 'ad hoc teleworking'; distributed teams; and networked relationships among clients, contractors and other organisations. The guide also considers the rise of solutions that are aimed at making mobile workers more effective, and the appearance of 'touchdown' sites and 'hotdesking' in organisations.

Furthermore, job roles are changing, with mobile workers becoming more self-sufficient, as they can rely more on technology to help them; secretaries are moving to 'hub' roles dealing with groups of dispersed workers; and, similarly, managers too are 'walking the job electronically' with less face to face contact with their staff.

main drivers

But the driver for change isn't just technology. Professionals across a broad range of sectors and jobs expect a lot more from their working lives these days. Not only do they expect to spend a lot more time 'unchained' from the traditional office environment, but they are demanding a lot more flexibility to balance their work and home lives.

It's no exaggeration to say that many professionals feel 'naked' without online access to their emails, at the very least, while they're on the move. And access to 'mission critical' applications, such as salesforce automation, a field engineering database or a live financial services quotation system, is becoming a differentiator for business success.

A salesperson, for example, who spends more time on admin in the office than out and about meeting clients face to face is unlikely to be a top performer. That's long been the case – but now the tools to back up mobile working mean there is no excuse for not maximising work effort for professionals who spend some or all of their time out of the office.

The other driver comes from government and health campaigners. The workplace has seen a rising tide of stress-related illnesses in recent years – issues such as lack of control, pace of change and external pressures such as debt and family problems are all involved in a complex, 'psycho-social' mix leading to high absenteeism and low productivity and morale.

Part of the answer in solving stress problems is in flexibility, such as allowing employees to adapt their working hours and place of work. The government has set certain objectives through regulation that includes the Working Time Directive and flexible arrangements for parents and carers. But enlightened employers are recognising that technology such as wireless computing can be combined with flexible working arrangements to mutual benefit – although there can be a downside (see later).

A related example of technology helping to improve employee wellbeing is the Home Computing Initiatives (HCI), a government scheme that allows organisations to loan computers to employees for home use as a tax free benefit. The idea is to give people access to decent, well maintained home computers to use for work, educational and entertainment activities, helping them to learn more about IT and improve their productivity and morale in the workplace. A computer can be combined with a wireless home network for extra flexibility in placing the equipment and communicating on the Internet. See the IoD publication *Fit for the Future* for more details.

in the office

An area ripe for more investigation in many companies is increasing flexibility in the use of office space. As the *Flexible Working Guide* notes, many office-based organisations suffer the paradox of apparently inadequate office space and facilities, yet low building utilisation – the reason being that offices are usually designed as if every employee was always there.

Many larger firms have introduced touchdown points and hotdesking in offices for workers who are visiting other offices or who don't really need a permanent desk of their own. When armed with a wireless enabled notebook computer, and with suitable wireless in-house network, logging in to the office network is then a breeze for such workers. Wireless computing is also ideal for meeting rooms and other communal areas.

Similarly, the rise of business centres (such as those run by Regus) and those in locations such as airports and motorway service stations offer other touchdown opportunities for businesspeople.

But for many firms the solution to making the most out of office space will involve close examination of work processes, setting up, for example, temporary co-location of project teams, more shared facilities and streamlining communications.

a downside to flexibility?

There are several concerns about the growth of mobile working and flexibility that should be addressed.

Training and support for the use of mobile technology is often under-resourced. Employees endure enough frustrations in the office and shouldn't have more trouble on the road or at home. This is also a question of productivity – poorly designed mobile solutions simply won't get used to their full potential – a salesforce system, for example, has to tie in with the core motivation of salespeople or they may not enter the data that 'head office' needs. Designers must involve users in mobile systems.

A potentially more serious issue is the impact on work-life balance. While technology can free people to work as and where they like, it may also create extra pressure to complete work out of working hours, outweighing the very advantages it is supposed to bring. There are very real fears of never being away from work, and of information overload. This is already a function of Britain's 'presenteeism' culture and long working hours, and it may well be that mobile technology could exacerbate a trend that is already there, particularly in some industries with a 'macho' image such as financial services. Workplace stress certainly can't be solved by technology solutions alone – working practices and processes need to be looked at in the round.

Allied to this is an understandable fear among managers that they will lose control over staff spending much of the working week away from the office. There are also fears that staff won't be as accessible to clients, although this is one factor that good quality mobile technology can handle almost as well as being stationed at head office. There's no doubt that the skills needed to be an excellent 'virtual manager' will grow in importance – these include excellent communications skills and good relationship building, and a dominant issue is trust. It is possible to map out the characteristics of high and low trust teamworking – see the booklet *What makes an excellent virtual manager* from Roffey Park Institute for details.

WORKING AND WIRELESS TRENDS

☐ **more hours on the road**
Professionals are spending an increasing proportion of their time outside the office – from 25% of working hours two years ago, to an anticipated 42% in two years' time.

☐ **no such thing as a typical working day**
Work day patterns are becoming increasingly fragmented as a result of globalisation.

☐ **virtual workplace relationships common**
Business people increasingly work in virtual teams across geographies.

☐ **communication is the main out-of-office activity**
The most common work performed outside the office is communication with colleagues and business contacts, whether in face-to-face meetings, by phone or via email.

☐ **productivity is high**
Business professionals have been quick to embrace the shift towards greater mobility, with the majority feeling as or more productive working outside the office as within.

☐ **mobile working delivers significant business benefits**
The majority of professionals see mobile working and wireless technology delivering significant competitive advantage.

☐ **wireless technology increasingly pervasive**
A majority of professionals own a laptop and wireless hotspot usage is a growing trend.

☐ **control over professional and personal lives**
Three-quarters of professionals believe mobile working allows them greater control over their professional lives and 60% perceive benefits in managing their personal lives.

☐ **barriers to mobile working**
Security concerns and cost top the list of reasons companies cite for not encouraging more mobile working.

☐ **EU to boost mobile working**
The majority of respondents see EU enlargement as a future driver of mobile working.

Source: Destination Wireless survey, Economist Intelligence Unit for Intel.

In looking at the needs of employees for flexibility, it is clear that a range of solutions may need to be applied to avoid the possibility of raising stress levels. Not only do different types of work need different solutions, but as the *Complete Guide to Flexible Working* notes: "Many people have requirements that change during the working day – formal meetings, communicating by phone, concentrated study and relaxed discussions..."

So flexible and remote working is a complex business – all sorts of issues arise – such as potential loss of control for managers, what types or applications to deploy on a mobile basis, virtual teamworking, how to measure productivity and return on investment. But there is no going back from the 'office exodus' – quite the reverse, as the trend for more flexibility will only gather pace.

FLEXIBLE LAWYERS

"It's been the most popular thing we've introduced for a long time," is how Paul Greenwood, chief information officer at law firm Clifford Chance, describes the firm's wireless computing initiative. Through a combination of home Wi-Fi installations and a wireless-based private network sourced from Equant, a subsidiary of France Telecom, the firm's top lawyers can access their email wherever they happen to be.

While on the move, lawyers use BlackBerry handheld devices to read email. The small screens aren't ideal for displaying attachments, concedes Greenwood, but they still provide enough information to be useful. At the very least, he points out, the BlackBerry acts as a prompt to let you know if you have to go to a computer and download a document to print out. And, of course, many emails don't have attachments and can be dealt with directly from the BlackBerry.

At home, Wi-Fi enables lawyers to keep in touch without intruding any more than is necessary on their personal life. "They can be part of the family, and work without detaching themselves from family life," is how Greenwood describes it. "We're a hard-working culture where the form of occupation makes significant demands on your personal time, and wireless computing has helped people to make best use of that time."

the wider picture

To get the most out of wireless computing, companies need to know how it can be complemented and supported by other communication technologies, says Marc Beishon, business and technology writer

As outlined in chapter 1, wireless computing represents a significant technological advance. However, it isn't the only show in town. Rather, it should be viewed as a key complementary communications tool, alongside mobile phone networks and fixed-line communications.

the growth of broadband

In particular so-called 'broadband' rollouts are now becoming very popular in smaller business and in homes. This is crucial, as at the end of any broadband connection can lie a local wireless network. As the Department of Trade and Industry says: "Wi-Fi local networks are a perfect complement to broadband for small businesses."

After a slow start, the UK is now much better provided for in broadband availability. Broadband via ADSL, for example, is now available to 80 per cent of UK households, and is predicted to rise to 90 per cent in the next year, if local demand holds up. Broadband

EXECUTIVE SUMMARY

- [ ] broadband Internet connections are a key driver for wireless computing at work and at home
- [ ] the OECD has named the UK as a leading proponent in the rollout of broadband Internet services
- [ ] although GPRS and 3G mobile phone networks cannot match the speed of connection of Wi-Fi, they do offer extensive coverage
- [ ] companies cite accessing data on the move and improving work/life balance as key wireless benefits
- [ ] developing a wireless strategy is critical to maximising effectiveness and cost optimisation

via cable is available to around 45 per cent of UK households, though these are generally in areas where ADSL is also available. (Data from a Select Committee on Trade and Industry report on broadband.)

Indeed, the Organisation of Economic Co-operation and Development (OECD) has recently tipped Britain to be one of the world leaders in the rollout of broadband Internet services. It suggests that BT could better the 90 per cent ADSL figure quoted above to 99 per cent by next year.

impact on business

In the business world, a membership survey by the British Chambers of Commerce (BCC) found that 39 per cent of companies now have broadband. This is an increase of more than 100 per cent on the previous year's survey. Of those businesses yet to get on the broadband wagon, 60.9 per cent "think they will be pressured by their customers and suppliers into adopting it within five years, and 46 per cent would like to access it but are based in areas where it is not available".

Based on the findings of one of its recent surveys, Cable firm NTL estimates that more than half (56 per cent) of the UK's small businesses have upgraded to broadband, with Scottish firms leading the country with 62 per cent. NTL also says that companies are recovering a 'mammoth' 52 days a year in lost productivity, with two thirds of the respondents saying that broadband had significantly improved their ability to communicate effectively with customers and suppliers. Furthermore, half identified the ability to implement new business applications as a key advantage.

The survey also revealed that more than two thirds of executives use the time saved by broadband for marketing and new business initiatives instead of reducing their working hours. However, over one third of respondents felt broadband offered no tangible advantage to their business – which may suggest that some firms may be slow to discover new ways of working.

And yet, according to Oftel, the overall number of UK households and small businesses connecting to the Internet via a broadband connection has passed the three million mark, and more than 40,000 households and businesses a week are said to be installing an 'always-on' Internet connection.

Wireless operators are also helping in the rush to provide broadband services to remote areas, and offering more competition in areas already partly provisioned. Community wireless broadband providers, such as South Oxfordshire Broadband, are helping people get broadband speeds in their home and businesses even though they are outside ADSL or cable areas. The quality of village life these days needs to be matched with quality communications, especially for the many top professionals flocking to semi-rural locations.

NTL is putting in a transmitter with a 10km range in Milton Keynes, which has a poor communications infrastructure for a 'new town'. With satellite also offering a broadband route, few will be left to complain that they won't be part of the Internet revolution in a few years' time.

the role of mobile phones

The other key technology is the mobile phone, which has all but reached a saturation level of rollout in the UK, at least for basic voice phones.

The much vaunted 3G (third generation) networks – after a long and very expensive gestation – look set for wide deployment this year. While they won't offer the speed of a Wi-Fi connection, they will have the key advantage of extensive coverage. Indeed, one core use of a cell phone will be to tell you when you're in range of a Wi-Fi hotspot.

The existing GSM and GPRS digital cell phone networks are fine for sending and receiving relatively small amounts of data. And, analysts are predicting an interesting convergence of Wi-Fi and mobile phone usage, with dual purpose notebook computers and other devices already in use by some of the advance techno-guard.

wireless take-up

Data on wireless computing take-up is more difficult to come by, Britain is still very much in the early adopter stage. The market can be broken down into:

☐ the number of wireless networks in use in companies (probably about ten per cent of businesses so far)

Are you qualified to be a director?

EXECUTIVE DIRECTOR

FTSE 100 company wishes to appoint a Marketing Director to the board. The candidate must either be cogniscent with all aspects of company direction and hold the IoD Diploma in Company Direction or undertake the programme on appointment. All current members of the board are Chartered Directors and it is expected that the successful candidate will progress to C Dir status.

FINANCE DIRECTOR

Medium sized organisation seeks a qualified accountant who as a member of the board is also able to make a significant contribution to the overall development of the business. Accordingly, a Chartered Director is preferred, identifying a demonstrable track record of success in delivering profitable growth.

CHAIRMAN

International company requires a Chairman to lead investor relations and present to key financial institutions. The successful candidate will hold the IoD Diploma in Company Direction and be a Chartered Director, due to the high regard for these qualifications in the investment community.

NON-EXECUTIVE DIRECTOR

A major PLC is looking to expand its board with an experienced NED. The candidate must be a Chartered Director and therefore demonstrate the highest levels of strategic direction and the profile to communicate with shareholders.

CHIEF EXECUTIVE

This not for profit organisation is seeking an experienced chief executive possessing high standards of leadership and ability to guide the organisation through a period of restructuring and regional expansion. In addition, knowledge of and adherence to, sound corporate governance is essential. Only Chartered Directors will be considered for this position.

COMPANY SECRETARY

A FTSE 50 organisation seeks a company secretary who can demonstrate the experience and confidence to work with a high profile main board consisting of Chartered Directors. The successful candidate is also expected to contribute to the strategic direction of the company and be a senior team leader. Preference will be given to a Chartered Secretary who has also qualified as a Chartered Director.

These positions are fictitious but are representative of Chartered Directors and their organisations

Chartered Director is the IoD's professional qualification for directors and receives the endorsement and support of government, regulators, the investment community, executive search agencies, the public sector and organisations including FTSE 100 companies.

To read some of the most recent Chartered Director success stories, visit www.iod.com/chartered

Please quote reference DG04   E chartered.director@iod.com   T 020 7766 2601

☐   the number of public wireless 'hotspots' (now about 7,000 in the UK)

☐   the number of wireless networks in use in homes

UK figures on home use are hard to obtain – but a worldwide report from In-Stat /MDR found that in 2003 the home Wi-Fi market achieved 'staggering growth', jumping to 22.7m units. This represents a 214 per cent increase from 2002's 7.2m units. Home Wi-Fi is also connecting people's computers to entertainment systems, as well as providing a convenient way of accessing the Internet around the house for personal and business use (see chapter 7). Broadband Internet connections are a key driver.

As for public 'hotspots', a recent survey by Intel to locate Britain's technology hub identified Exeter as the capital of Britain's Wi-Fi revolution, followed by Bangor and Newcastle. It also found that more of the UK's hotspots are located in pubs than anywhere else. BT Openzone, meanwhile, is busy installing access points in more than 500 McDonald's restaurants, so it could be a close run thing between burgers and beer.

As for the future, research group IDC expects the number of Western European wireless hotspots to grow to more than 32,500 locations by 2007 (and to generate total revenue of $1.4bn).

future challenges

There is both opportunity and challenge in extending wireless connectivity once the broadband link is available at any point, from office, to hotspot, to home. According to a recent survey by the IoD and Toshiba, most firms are presently in the position of believing that wireless working can provide business advantage, but only 21 per cent of respondents actually have a strategy to discover why and how wireless can be used effectively in the business.

The main advantages cited by the vast majority of respondents for wireless working are accessing corporate data on the move and empowering employees to achieve better productivity and work-life balance. To this extent, many firms are seeing the 'big picture'. However, for some, simply enjoying the lower costs and flexibility of an 'unwired' office may be the more obvious direct benefits.

But a widespread lack of process and strategy is a problem. The key is to take a step back and review procedures for implementing existing and new wireless systems to avoid poor effectiveness and lack of cost optimisation, not to mention possible security breaches.

Analysts are now looking in detail at the type of wireless application that is being rolled out by companies in the last few months. Meta Group is seeing action in 'targeted field-force automation' (eg. route delivery, service, field sales, asset management) "that is an extension of an existing environment, rather than general-purpose mobile infrastructure".

Meta also expects more than 50 per cent of enterprises to have wireless email in place within two to three years. This will "often lead to more wireless applications as users see the value in mobility solutions", although a knock on effect will be to place pressure on IT departments to support users on various devices, such as notebooks, tablet PCs, PDAs and smart phones, and with various connections, such as Wi-Fi and mobile phones.

Another analyst, IDC, also considers that mobilising workforces will "largely depend on the availability of industry-tailored solutions". That's because 'considerable disparities' exist between companies in different vertical sectors, in terms of factors such as worker mobility patterns, primary mobile application usage, advanced features such as biometrics and asset tracking, and primary deployment concerns, such as cost and security. 'One size fits all' solutions are unlikely to meet the diverse needs of mobile enterprises, says IDC.

The foundations are now in place for most companies to both join the broadband age and enjoy wireless working. The next few years will see many successes – and failures – in wireless mobility, but those with an appreciation of the services on offer and a solid strategy will do best (see box).

SIX STEPS TO A SUCCESSFUL WIRELESS STRATEGY

☐ **step one – assess the wireless needs of your workforce**
The first step is to look at exactly what wireless technology your organisation needs. It is pointless investing in wireless products if the business has no field-working, hot-desking or mobile communication requirements. Look at what benefits wireless technology will offer to the workforce. Will it make them more productive? Will employees benefit from flexible working or wireless access at home? If the answer is yes, then wireless computing could make a sound investment.

☐ **step two – plan wireless technology investments according to your needs**
Don't get carried away with buying the latest technology for the sake of it but invest dependent on your needs. Too many companies buy the latest devices without thinking about whether they really need it. Do you need a compact wireless device for basic computing functions? Buy a PDA. Do you require something altogether more powerful? Then a notebook PC could meet your needs. Decide who needs wireless computing and what they need it for and make your technology investments accordingly.

☐ **step three – implement wireless working policies**
Successful implementation is only one part of the jigsaw. It is essential that businesses implement wireless working policies to ensure they are guiding their workforce on how to get the most out of technology. Policies aren't about showing users where the on-switch is. They are designed to offer guidance on when, where and how they should be working. The risk of 'anytime/anywhere' connectivity is that users can feel they're expected to work 'everywhere/all the time'. Policies are designed to ensure businesses gain improved employee productivity and get the work-life balance right.

☐ **step four – educate and train users**
After buying the technology, it's vital that users receive both education and training. Too many businesses leave the users to get on with it, without any formal guidance. Users need to know how to use wireless – and what benefits it can truly offer.

☐ **step five – implement security technology**
Security is quite rightly still a huge concern surrounding the implementation of wireless networks – and an issue that's ignored by many businesses. An insecure wireless network can open the business up to hacker and virus attacks or data theft. Businesses need to ensure they put security architecture in place that includes a virtual private network (VPN) and firewall technology.

☐ **step six – provide comprehensive support**
Many firms make the mistake of thinking that their wireless planning ends when implementation is complete. Service and support are often overlooked and subsequently, problems with wireless technology become difficult to resolve. It is essential for firms to ensure that all service and support staff are Wi-Fi and Bluetooth trained, or at the very least that the business has access to trained personnel from an external source.

maximising return on investment

Deciding whether to invest in wireless technology – and where to invest – isn't easy, but there are some guidelines for businesses, says Sally Whittle, business and technology writer

The key to getting the maximum value from any project is getting three basics right: the application, the network and the management.

the application

Experts have identified certain applications where wireless technology will generally deliver the biggest, and fastest benefits. These 'sweet spots' include providing warehouse staff with wireless access to inventory applications. In most cases, warehouses don't have access to the corporate network, so providing wireless access to inventory data can make stock reporting much more accurate and reduce the time taken to meet customer orders.

EXECUTIVE SUMMARY

☐ the best wireless projects save businesses time and avoid wasted effort

☐ with Wi-FI, there's no need to invest heavily in network devices and connectivity technology

☐ people issues are paramount – neglecting the effect that new technologies will have on staff and the way they work can lead to resentment and inefficiency

Another 'sweet spot' involves providing sales staff with the technology to access Wi-Fi hotspots so that they can check stock levels and file new customer orders while they are still out in the field. In many companies, new orders aren't processed until sales staff return to head office, or orders are submitted by fax and entered manually into the computer systems.

As well as offering convenience, wireless technology can boost productivity. According to technology analyst Forrester Research, 60 per cent of companies using wireless technology report higher productivity and 40 per cent see improved customer service. An additional 20 per cent say wireless has enabled their business to improve logistics. It makes sense that an engineer who is able to fill in fault reports on site and order spare parts immediately will be able to finish more repairs in a day. Customers appreciate dealing with sales staff who can answer questions on the spot, and sales staff will be more motivated as a result.

The best wireless projects save businesses time and avoid wasted effort. At supermarket chain Tesco, for example, staff working in the store use a wireless network to check whether particular items are available in the stock room – and where in the stock room products are. As a result, empty shelves get filled faster, and customers are happier.

the network

Having chosen the right application for wireless access, managers must choose from a bewildering choice of network devices and connectivity technologies. A company can spend tens of thousands of pounds on high-end laptops with fast, GPRS modems that communicate over mobile phone networks. However, it's also possible to deliver high-speed wireless access quickly and cost-effectively using Wi-Fi networks.

Wi-Fi networks are ideal where workers are accessing the corporate network from in the office and at home. Installing Wi-Fi access for homeworkers can cost less than £150 per employee or per Wi-Fi access system, and the network is extremely simple to maintain. Wi-Fi is also a highly cost-effective way to provide access for workers on the road, who can access the network using hotspots in places such as hotels, motorway service stations, airports and coffee bars.

management

All of the issues covered so far are crucial, but just as big a factor to consider is change management. You're asking your employees to work differently. Have you asked them how they feel about this? And, how are you going to help

CASE STUDY: SCOTTISH WATER

When your field engineer force has to cover a third of the UK the last thing you want them doing is going to the wrong address, with the wrong information, and at the wrong time.

But that was just what was happening at Scottish Water two years ago. The company was formed that year through the merger of a number of smaller power and utility companies, and a key part of the new company's strategy was to reduce operating costs by 40 per cent before 2006.

Such a formidable challenge might have defeated the organisation if it hadn't been for wireless and mobile technology, says Sheryl Black, Scottish Water's customer service director. "We had to think differently."

Scottish Water rolled out a field sales application based on Oracle customer relationship management (CRM) software. More than 200 engineers working in the field now access the software using specially ruggedised laptop computers.

This gives them immediate access to the customer management system and a geographic information application that helps engineers reach customers quickly and deal with problems efficiently.

Scottish Water spent £2m on software for the project, £1.9m on implementation and management, plus over £3m on a change management programme to support the technology, making a £7m total investment. But, says Black, the project has already delivered a full return on investment. "We've already taken £18m out of costs within one year's use of this system, and are predicting a return on investment of 250 per cent over three years."

Other benefits include sharper prioritisation of tasks, increased jobs per day – from five to 11 on average, sharp cuts in both overtime and downtime, and because of better field operations, calls to contact centres now get resolved in the first call 85 per cent of the time, instead of 40 per cent.

"Mobile is the glue of this system and saves us all so much time. Anyone with a field force should be looking at this," says Black.

them to adapt to the new system? Cultural issues and good training and support during the rollout matter as much, if not more, than the choice of specific network or handheld technologies.

For example, when T-Mobile rolled out wireless networking to its engineers, the company was able to automatically allocate jobs to workers based on their location. This improved efficiency dramatically, but meant that engineers could no longer choose their own schedule for the day. To avoid bad feeling, managers at the company ran special training courses to explain the point of the wireless technology, and its benefits.

CASE STUDY: ITN

TV news producer ITN has recently rolled out a Wi-Fi network from Telindus in three of its London offices. Using wireless has reduced the amount of time taken to prepare for news broadcasts, and allowed journalists at ITN to work more flexibly, making them more efficient.

The Wi-Fi network is available to staff working in two offices and the company's central London studio, so journalists can access the Internet even if they aren't at their desks. This is important because ITN's business depends on having fast access to information, explains Ian Auger, ITN's head of IT and communications. "The business is dictated by world events, and we often need to get equipment into a studio at very short notice," says Auger. "With Wi-Fi we can set things up quickly, without worrying that cables are going to get damaged."

The Wi-Fi network uses software from Trapeze and five network access points, which are extremely cost-effective. "The level of functionality that Wi-Fi offers, in relation to the cost, makes it a very good investment," he says.

Over the coming months, ITN hopes to extend the Wi-Fi network to cover all of the company's studios and news rooms, to allow staff to be completely mobile across the company.

As a rule of thumb, training and management add around 40 per cent to the total cost of any wireless project. Any cost-benefit analysis should factor this in, and also recognise that the IT department is now being asked to look after what could be very unfamiliar devices. Supporting a mobile or wireless worker can increase support costs by up to 60 per cent, according to analyst firm Gartner Group.

are benefits measurable?

Can you measure some of the benefits? The Wi-Fi Alliance, an advocacy organisation for wireless computing, has a benefits calculator that is accessible from its website (www.wi-fi.org), which attempts to calculate the return on investment based on the productivity gains associated with increased access to the corporate network.

The calculator comprises a spreadsheet into which you record the number of employees, and then specify how many are being considered for wireless, their salaries, time spent in meetings, time spent travelling with access to public Wi-Fi hotspots, costs associated with installing a wireless network, etc. Results are then presented in terms of money savings, or payback in months, relative to the up-front costs for installation and hardware and the recurring costs for IT support.

INVESTMENT ACTION POINTS

- ☐ save costs by choosing established products; the price of new mobile devices usually falls by 25 per cent in the first 12 months

- ☐ standardise. Allowing employees to choose their own laptops, phones and PDAs will increase support costs enormously

- ☐ look for service discounts. Buying your handheld computers from your network operator, for example, may be cheaper than buying the two separately. Further discounts may be offered if you commit to the network for a set period

- ☐ buy more devices than you think you will need. Those spares will come in handy if the project is successful and needs to be expanded

the company wireless network

Wireless technologies offer companies savings on their IT investment, as well as greater flexibility and efficiency, reports Sally Whittle, business and technology writer

Advertisements for wireless technology often focus on how wireless users can access their email from the beach, or download the latest sales figures without leaving a customer site. However, according to research from analyst group In-Stat/MDR, the majority of wireless deployments take place inside offices.

In-Stat/MDR predicted in 2000 that wireless networks would become a 'non-negotiable' part of corporate IT deployment. This forecast is certainly borne out in a recent survey by the Economist Intelligence Unit, in which more than 80 per cent of respondents said wireless was beneficial for flexible working and has a "real impact on workforce productivity and team collaboration".

And there's a clear cost benefit. Building a wireless network inside your company's offices means that you won't need to lay new cables as your business grows. A typical Wi-Fi network can be up to 90 per cent cheaper than a conventional network. This is particularly good news for small companies as it means they can afford to extend access as they grow, without ripping up the floor to lay new cables.

EXECUTIVE SUMMARY

☐ wireless networks can help staff avoid 'down time' by enabling them to keep working and emailing while away from their desks

☐ RFID is a wireless technology that tracks the movement of stock in real-time, saving businesses millions in lost stock and inventory costs

☐ businesses need to take security seriously, investing in specialist encryption software to protect themselves

---

CASE STUDY: THAMESIDE COUNCIL

Thameside Council has been using Wi-Fi since September 2003, and is now expanding the technology to all 1,500 of its employees.

The council bought a complete Wi-Fi solution from wireless specialist Trapeze, initially to help ten key IT support workers to be more mobile. "The biggest challenge for us is that people are constantly moving jobs and moving desks, and that's very time-consuming if you need to switch cables and plug things in," explains Peter Faulkner, network team leader at Thameside.

The initial investment was less than £6,000 – still a substantial investment for the council. "It was quite expensive, but it gives us the potential to connect to up to 200 users as we expand the network," says Faulkner.

Staff accessing the wireless network do so simply by logging on to their desktop PC, and many don't even realise they are using a wireless connection. This invisibility was one of the key reasons for choosing wireless, since the council won't need any additional training, apart from that provided to IT support staff.

Configuring the network was extremely straightforward, using Trapeze's management software. "It let us draw up a floor plan showing where people would work and even information about the walls' construction materials, and then showed us exactly where we needed access points and how many," says Faulkner. "It's not necessarily faster than the wired network, but it's far more flexible and the whole project has been extremely successful."

---

efficiency gains

Research conducted by Microsoft in 2004 suggests that there are other cost-benefits to using wireless in the office. Using a wireless network to take notes and send email from meeting rooms saved office workers an average 213 hours over one year, equivalent to a $13,000 saving.

So, the low cost of wireless makes it cost-effective to extend access to parts of your building that aren't used regularly – such as the conference and meeting rooms that Microsoft has identified. Similarly, at Lewisham Borough Council in London, knowledge workers who spend a lot of time in meetings have been provided with a Wi-Fi network, allowing them to take notes and send emails while they are away from their desks.

And, Sandwell Hospital – part of the Sandwell and West Birmingham NHS Trust – has fitted Wi-Fi access points in 20 hospital wards. These allow doctors and pharmacy staff to access medical databases, and issue prescriptions at the

> ### POTENTIAL USES OF WI-FI
>
> ☐ replacing fixed wiring or installing a network in an office. While a lot of modern offices may already be wired with a computer network, a lot of older premises are not ideal places to install wiring, and cabling can be expensive and time consuming to put in. Wireless equipment is an straightforward alternative, and also allows offices to be rearranged with minimal fuss
>
> ☐ enabling access around the company – employees can take their laptops into meetings and get their latest emails and reports throughout the meeting. Another application could be setting up a training room for 'e-learning' – employees can take their laptops in and get started without wires
>
> ☐ flexible 'touchdown' points – workers who don't need permanent desks can go straight to a shared desk with a phone and wireless link straight to the office network
>
> ☐ on the shop floor – industrial environments are particularly tricky and potentially dangerous places for lots of wires – a wireless network gives workers freedom to use handheld terminals and computers in and around the building, reporting on assembly lines, for example
>
> ☐ on the retail floor – companies with retail environments such as shops and restaurants can install Wi-Fi to communicate with handheld stock control and meal ordering terminals
>
> ☐ running demos – a wireless adapter plugged into a network can make setting up demos and presentations in any room easy, with no worry about data cables. A wireless demo kit could also be taken to a customer site
>
> ☐ setting up temporary offices – construction companies, for example, often need temporary accommodation – a wireless network can cut costs and improve flexible working at a site. Another scenario might be setting up a stand at a trade show

bedside. This has reduced the average time taken to process a prescription by over an hour, and dramatically reduced the risk of errors in patients' medication.

the value of tracking devices

Wireless technologies can also be used to track the movement of stock in real-time, providing a whole new source of information. A wireless technology called RFID (radio frequency identification) was recently used to track runners in the New York marathon. Athletes fixed a small RFID tag to their shoe, where it emitted a radio signal. The signal was picked up by receiving devices placed along the route, and entered into a database. The result was a service that allowed anyone with Internet access to track the times and positions of any athlete in the race.

The same technology is being used in the UK by retailers including Marks & Spencer and Tesco to keep track of stock as it moves from supplier to distributor to the shop floor. The RFID tags cost less than 50 pence each, and can save companies millions of pounds in lost stock and inventory costs.

carrying out a cost analysis

If you are considering wireless-enabling your office premises, it's important to factor in all the costs. Although a Wi-Fi-enabled laptop or network may cost a few hundred pounds, companies also need to make sure the network will offer the necessary levels of performance, scalability and security.

To ensure the network delivers the right level of performance, you need to factor in how many people will be using it, and how much data will be travelling across it at peak times. It's not enough to simply install Wi-Fi access points at 100 metre intervals: if 20 people are accessing multimedia files through each access point, the network is likely to grind to a halt pretty quickly.

Management software is available to monitor the performance of a wireless network, and ensure the right applications and users are given priority. This software will also authenticate people trying to access the network and make sure that any policies applied on the corporate network (for example application access privileges) are extended to wireless users.

encryption software offers security

One of the biggest issues for any business considering rolling out wireless technology will be security. The most important advice is not to rely on the security features that come as standard with Wi-Fi and other wireless products, since hackers can easily penetrate these systems. Instead, security experts advice companies to invest in specialist security software that encrypts all information at both ends of the network, and while it is travelling across the connection.

hailing the hotspot

Public 'hotspots' are springing up everywhere, with an estimated 20,000 currently available worldwide. Sally Whittle, business and technology writer, takes a look at this new trend and its impact on businesses

One of the fastest growing uses of Wi-Fi is the public Wi-Fi service – also known as a 'hotspot'. Hotspots allow anyone within an area to access the Internet using a shared service. For example, a Wi-Fi user enjoying a coffee in the Borders bookstore on London's Oxford Street can access the Internet using a hotspot provided by Westminster City Council's tourist information service.

accessing hotspots

To access a public hotspot, all you need is a laptop or other computing device with Wi-Fi capability. With new laptops this will probably be built in, but otherwise PC cards that slot into your laptop can be bought at any electronics store starting from under £50. If a hotspot is being run as a commercial service for subscribers you may need to open an account. This will provide you with a password or access card to access the service.

To build a hotspot, you need to install one or more access points – boxes that can be attached to a wall or ceiling, and which provide network access to authorised users anywhere within a few hundred feet of the access point. One access point has a total bandwidth of around 20 times the speed of a typical home broadband connection.

EXECUTIVE SUMMARY

- [ ] hotspots provide fast Internet access in places where it wouldn't otherwise be possible
- [ ] most suppliers will work with clients to determine how many access points will be required and the best place to position them
- [ ] some UK businesses are setting up hotspots to gain competitive advantage. There are also community hotspots provided by not-for-profit organisations

WI-FI HOTSPOTS IN THE UK

- [ ] BT Openzone – BT has one of the UK's biggest networks of hotspots, with 2,000 across the UK. BT hotspots can be found at motorway service stations, hotels and phone kiosks in most major cities. (www.btopenzone.com)

- [ ] Boingo – Boingo is a network of independently owned hotspots that can all be accessed using a single account. So far, there are more than 6,000 hotspots worldwide, with 126 in the UK, many of them in Best Western hotels and branches of Café Nero. (www.boingo.com)

- [ ] T-Mobile – the mobile network operator offers access to a network of 250 UK hotspots in Starbucks coffee shops and selected Texaco petrol stations. Globally, T-Mobile is one of the world's biggest operators, with over 4,000 sites

Depending on the number of access points used, hotspots can be as small as a single Starbucks or as large as an airport lounge or library. Most Wi-Fi suppliers will provide customers with software that helps them calculate how many access points will be required to cover a particular area, and where the access points should be located for the best coverage.

main benefits of hotspots

The biggest benefit of hotspots is that they provide fast Internet access in places where it wouldn't otherwise be straightforward. One of the most popular locations for hotspots is in airport lounges, where business travellers could otherwise be waiting without access to email. Hotspots are also proving to be popular on college campuses, allowing students to access the university network and study outside the library.

However, hotspots are far from ubiquitous, and business users cannot rely on there being Wi-Fi access available 24 hours a day. That said, for workers in major cities things are beginning to improve. Analyst Gartner Group predicts that by the end of this year, there will be 24,000 hotspots worldwide, up from 10,000 last year.

Many of these are what Gartner calls 'community hotspots' – Wi-Fi services provided in town centre squares and other public areas by councils, or home-owners who share high-speed connections with their neighbours.

Some UK businesses are already using hotspots to generate competitive advantage. In the UK, Tottenham Hotspur Football Club has built a Wi-Fi network so that fans and staff can access the Internet during matches. The club hopes that the service, called Spurs Connect, will encourage corporate clients to use the ground more often.

Wi-Fi hotspots can also be a cost-effective option when organisations are providing Internet access in an area for the first time. When the Great Ormond Street hospital wanted to provide Internet access for young patients attending the hospital's school, a Wi-Fi hotspot was 90 per cent cheaper than creating a new, cabled network. With Wi-Fi it is also possible to extend Internet access to patients who are bed-bound and, therefore can't go to the classroom.

drawbacks to be addressed

There are some limitations that hotspot users should be aware of. For example, most hotspots are owned and operated by one company, with its own tariff and payment system. If a user moves out of that hotspot and into another, they will usually need a new account and payment system for that hotspot. This lack of 'roaming' makes it difficult to make the most of Wi-Fi – it's like having a separate mobile phone number and account for every country you visit.

The good news is that businesses are starting to address the issue. Boingo Wireless, for example, has agreements with 1,200 hotspot operators so that customers can access any of its hotspots using a single account and password. Currently, there are Boingo hotspots in the UK, US and some parts of Europe.

For businesses, the biggest concern about hotspots is security. When hotspots were first rolled out, there were a number of high-profile stories about 'drive-by' hacking, where unauthorised users were able to hack into wireless networks. The good news is that most hotspots are now well-protected, using virtual private networking technology that protects data by creating a virtual 'tunnel' as it travels across the Internet.

In addition, companies such as iPass provide businesses with software to ensure that employees can use public hotspots without compromising the company's data or networks.

CASE STUDY: CROWN PLAZA HOTEL

At the Crown Plaza hotel in the City of London, high-speed wireless access isn't an optional extra – it's just part of the service. "Today, when guests check into a five-star hotel they expect a high-speed wireless service," explains Veronica Pillon, the Crown Plaza's systems manager. "It's a necessity if you want to remain competitive."

The hotel's clientele is mainly business travellers and the hotel is often used for business meetings, so it has built hotspots to cover the lobby, restaurant and bar. In addition, all the guest rooms have Wi-Fi access points fitted as standard. To access the network, guests purchase an access card from the hotel's front desk, which provides 15 minutes access for around £5.

The hotel uses technology from wireless specialist Quadriga together with standard security and antivirus software to keep the network secure. "We've found that the wireless companies we've worked with have strong technical support and our supplier even offers a helpline for guests if they have problems," she says.

Pillon says that keeping the hotspot running has been surprisingly easy, and simpler than a comparable wired network. "Once it was installed and we'd trained the staff in using it, the biggest problem really has been when guests forget their cable to charge their laptops," she says.

wireless in the home

Malcolm Wheatley, business and technology writer, assesses the reasons behind the growing interest in wireless computing in the home

Even four or five years ago, the idea of wireless computing in the home would have seemed faintly ludicrous. But today the idea no longer seems so risible, with consumer-oriented outlets such as PC World stocking the technology in abundance, at affordable prices. Up and down Britain, perfectly ordinary homes are now wireless-enabled.

reasons to be cheerful

Finding the reasons why isn't difficult. Wireless in the home meets not just one need, but several. Even better still, wireless in the home complements technologies such as broadband and Intel's Centrino, which wireless-enables laptop computers. Buy into one technology, and the arguments in favour of the others immediately become more compelling.

EXECUTIVE SUMMARY

- [ ] wireless in the home supports the growing trend in flexible working
- [ ] it makes home working less intrusive, since laptop users can boot up anywhere, including the garden shed
- [ ] wireless technologies are enabling rural communities to take advantage of broadband connections to the Internet for the first time

So why is wireless in the home proving so popular? One reason, for sure, is the move to home-based working – either by corporate employees choosing to work occasionally at home, or by the increasingly technology-literate home-based self-employed. For them, wireless computing offers improvements in productivity, convenience and lifestyle.

living and working in the same space

Take the perennial problem of reconciling the needs of living space and working space. However cunningly furniture-makers design their wares, home computing equipment inevitably stamps a sizeable footprint on most homes. Owners of large executive homes may be able to set a study aside for the purpose, but most people shoehorn it in where it will fit.

Often this means compromising the 'feel' of the living space by, for example, parking a computer and laser printer in an otherwise elegant dining room, or squeezing it in a place that is not really ideal for work purposes, such as in the same room as the television. Wireless computing offers the best of both worlds: bulky hardware such as printers and large monitors can be tucked away in less obtrusive spots, while the laptop-bearing worker switches on wherever it's convenient – in the garden, on the patio, at the dining room table, or even in bed.

The impact is twofold. First, working at home is less intrusive in terms of its impact on family life. And second – perhaps because it is less intrusive – working at home becomes a much more realistic option. This in turn makes employees more productive: Microsoft, for example, which actively encourages employees to set up wireless computing capabilities at home, has seen a culture of home-based email 'triage' taking root. Before employees reach the office in the morning, most of their in-box will have been dealt with, either during the preceding evening or over breakfast.

supporting flexible working

Wireless in the home also meets a need for flexible working. BT has 63,000 flexible workers, around 10,000 of whom use wireless computing, says Chris Webber, head of 'agility' within BT Retail's Workstyle division. Danny MacLaughlin, head of one of BT's largest divisions, is a typical case in point. He's constantly travelling throughout the UK, so doesn't have a designated office in BT. Instead he either works from home or at 'hot desks' in BT buildings wherever he happens to be.

And executives such as MacLaughlin are increasingly regarded as role models. A recent survey of white collar workers, sponsored by the DTI, found that 93 per cent of women and 81 per cent of male employees wanted more freedom to work flexibly. Half of the respondents indicated that they felt their jobs were preventing them from being as involved in family life as they would wish. Worryingly, a third of respondents also expressed the view that their employers were not committed to helping them achieve a reasonable work-life balance.

that's entertainment

And increasingly, 'life' means entertainment. Today, a huge proportion of people's time and money is given over to leisure. The Internet revolution has meant that for millions of people, the Web is a leisure destination. Game-playing, casual surfing, bulletin boards, virtual groups, education, on-line shopping – millions of people now choose to spend time on-line instead of watching television, listening to music, or whatever else they used to do. And broadband, of course, has revolutionised the speed and power of that on-line leisure experience.

Now apply wireless technology. Instead of sitting in a study or other fixed location in a home, the on-line leisure experience can be enjoyed anywhere in the home. The 'router' that acts as the base unit is connected to the incoming broadband link, and, quite literally, the entire house and garden becomes broadband enabled. One technology has leveraged the strengths of another to create something that is more powerful than the sum of the two parts.

Wireless technology and the leisure dimension of computing also come together to create another benefit of wireless technology in the home: collective connectivity. The fact that wireless technology doesn't need cables makes it both simple and inexpensive to bring Internet connectivity to every member of the household. Adults can use it for work and on-line shopping, while children enjoy games, homework research or just casual surfing. With more and more children having personal computers in their bedrooms, wireless connectivity brings the Internet to their bedroom desks for very little extra expenditure.

connecting the countryside

The advantages outlined so far are ubiquitous. However, there are even greater benefits for people living in a rural location for whom conventional broadband access over the telephone line or cable system isn't feasible. For these

---

CASE STUDY: EDS

Having been used to a high speed Internet link up at work, Mateen Greenway, enterprise architect at London-based IT outsourcing giant EDS, was finding home Internet access speeds frustratingly slow. However, with the arrival of broadband, he took the opportunity to set-up a Wi-Fi hotspot at home.

Greenway now believes he is in the vanguard of a broad movement: "People just don't like large amounts of wire around the house," he says. His wife, for example, had barred him from extending the previous wire-based home network that he had beyond the first floor of the house.

Now, the entire house and garden are networked. "I can get office-level speed of access, wherever I am – in my office, or on the lawn," he enthuses. Better still, one broadband connection is shared among a number of personal computers, bringing the advantage of speed to the entire household.

---

people, wireless not only provides the means of communication within the home, but also provides the channel of communication out to the Internet. The radio 'footprint' is not just the home and garden, but the distance between the individual computers in the home and the nearest base station – creating, in effect, 'wireless communities'.

teleworking and home working

There is growing recognition of the contribution made to the economy by teleworkers and the home-based self-employed. As a result, a combination of grant aid and other incentives from bodies such as the European Union and regional development agencies have brought wireless-based broadband into remote and rural areas. A tie-up between BT and Scottish telecoms provider THUS, for example, has seen wireless technology pressed into service to bring high-speed Internet access to around a third of the population of the Western Isles, Orkney and Shetland.

Private companies are getting in on the act, too, often in partnership with local communities. Take the Hampshire village of Kingsclere, for example. The village is home to a number of businesses and consumers who were interested in broadband access, but still fell short of the 'trigger level' required by BT to upgrade the local exchange.

Undeterred, the community secured a £15,000 grant from the South East England Development Agency, and hired local internet service provider FDM Broadband to erect wireless base stations and bring high-speed Internet access to the village. So far, explains FDM's managing director Karl Crossman, three base stations are in operation and a fourth is due to be commissioned.

For an 'always on' broadband connection, users pay either £22.95 a month, or £99 a month, depending on the bandwidth capacity of the connection that they require. The village presently has 130 subscribers, explains Crossman, with 250 anticipated by the end of the year.

Even just a few years ago, the idea would have seemed akin to science fiction. But, in Britain, 2004 has seen science fiction become science fact.

understanding
mobile devices

Bryan Betts, business and technology writer, takes a look at the wide choice of mobile wireless devices available

Staying in touch on the move has never been easier, with a broad choice of devices to maintain access to your voice calls and emails, the Internet and just about anything else you may need. Getting wirelessly connected is more practical too, as public wireless networks called 'hotspots' pop up all around the world, and as greater numbers of organisations install their own wireless networks.

The main way of getting connected for most mobile professionals is still a portable PC such as a laptop or notebook. These have the great advantage of being compatible with other PCs, so they can use the same software and they work the same way you are used to.

Most new notebooks have wireless connectivity built in, so they are ideal for remote working and increased productivity. Indeed, although some people still have a desktop PC as well, more of us are using a laptop as our sole PC device. Research firm META group predicts that by 2006 only 45 per cent of corporate users will cite a traditional desktop PC as their primary information device.

EXECUTIVE SUMMARY

☐ laptop PCs are great for anyone who types a lot, or needs a relatively large screen. They run standard PC software

☐ tablets use a touchscreen and a stylus so are useful for taking long-hand notes or sketching and sharing graphical concepts

☐ PDAs are pocket-sized and good for carrying information around in an accessible way. Most have wireless connectivity and built-in email

☐ smartphones combine a mobile phone and a PDA so they can connect from anywhere. Like PDAs they can synchronise with your PC diary. Also like PDAs, however, their small screens are a disadvantage for many office applications

---

WHAT IS BLUETOOTH?

Bluetooth is a wireless replacement for network cables – one of its uses is to connect mobile phones to laptops, PDAs and headsets. It can be used to connect a PC or PDA to a network but is much slower than Wi-Fi. Its range is much lower too, typically ten metres at most.

The advantage of Bluetooth is that your laptop can now connect to a mobile phone out of sight in your pocket or bag, or to a local wireless network since a few hotspots support Bluetooth as well as Wi-Fi.

You can even set up an office or home PC to share its network connection via a Bluetooth adapter. As well as allowing you to synchronise your Bluetooth-equipped PDA with the diary on the PC, this would enable the PDA to connect for email or web browsing too. Other devices such as printers can also connect wirelessly by Bluetooth.

Most portable PCs have keyboards but there is also a version called a tablet PC that has a touch-sensitive screen and software to recognise handwriting. Some tablet PCs have a keyboard too while others save weight by having only the touchscreen.

Although tablet PCs were not the huge initial success that Microsoft wanted, touchscreen PCs have long been popular for specific tasks such as filling in survey forms. Now that Microsoft has added handwriting recognition software, they are gaining new uses as electronic sketchpads and notepads; professionals are finding they are excellent for sharing graphical concepts, for example.

META group predicts that 40 per cent of us will use a laptop or tablet PC as our main device by 2006. Portable PCs can also be used in the office of course, sometimes with the addition of an external full-size keyboard, a mouse and an adjustable monitor. By making them more comfortable to use, these additions should satisfy the relevant health and safety rules too.

smaller and lighter devices

For the 15 per cent who need something smaller and lighter than a portable PC, the obvious choice is a personal digital assistant (PDA). The best known devices in this category are electronic organisers based on either the Palm software, such as Palm's own Tungsten devices and the Sony Clie range, or Microsoft's Pocket PC operating system, such as Toshiba's Pocket PC family and Hewlett Packard's iPaq range.

Most PDAs rely on a touchscreen and a stylus or pen for data entry, but a few have a tiny keyboard that you press with your thumbs while holding the device in both hands. Again, it is possible to add external keyboards that either clip onto the PDA, or talk to it via an infrared or Bluetooth short-range wireless connection.

PDAs have the great advantage that they were designed with portability in mind, and can keep you organised by synchronising with your PC's diary. They have since gained all the other necessities of modern business life, such as email and a web browser, and in some cases software to read and write SMS text messages.

There are also ways to connect PDAs to business software applications so that, for example, price lists or other key data can be downloaded. They can even be used by an IT manager to control full-size computers or scan for hackers and intruders on a network.

One thing PDAs cannot do is run PC software. Even those based on Microsoft Pocket PC need Windows programs to be altered somewhat, and although they look similar to Microsoft Windows, once you start using them you'll find they work differently. The other drawback is that the shift to power-hungry colour screens means that most PDAs now rely on rechargeable batteries. So, if your business trip is going to last a few days you'd better remember to take the battery charger.

connecting to networks and mobiles

Almost all portable PCs and PDAs now come with some kind of inbuilt network connection. Older models needed network cables but newer ones have a radio link such as Bluetooth or Wi-Fi. Using these radio links is relatively simple, requiring fewer cables and extra kit.

Many laptops, some PDAs such as Toshiba's Pocket PC e800, and even a few mobile phones – Nokia's newest Communicator, for example – have Wi-Fi built in. Alternatively, it can be added to most devices via a simple plug-in card or USB adapter.

The ability to connect over the mobile phone system, using the GPRS or 3G mobile phone networks, can also be added to a portable PC via a plug-in card.

Combination cards are now appearing which include both Wi-Fi – for fast connections in the office or at a public hotspot – and GPRS – which is slower but much more widely available.

Alternatively, PDAs and PCs can link to a separate mobile phone over Bluetooth and use it as if it were a modem. The plug-in GPRS card has the advantage of simplicity, while the Bluetooth route wins out when the best place for a strong mobile phone signal differs from the best place to type your email; so the phone could go on the hotel window sill and the PC on the desk.

Some PDAs also have a mobile phone built in for wireless connectivity when out and about, while conversely, some mobile phones now have a PDA built in. The result is a smartphone, which aims to combine the best of both worlds in a pocket-sized device.

limitations

Inevitably there are compromises. Smartphones that derive from PDAs and have touchscreens, such as the O₂ xda and Palm Treo, are easier to use as PDAs than phones, but they are but bulkier.

Meanwhile, those that derive from phones and rely on a numeric keypad for control, such as the Microsoft-based Orange SPV and Nokia's 3660 and 6600, are easier to use as phones but harder to put data into or write messages on.

How much this matters depends on what you will use the smartphone for. It will synchronise with your PC, just as a PDA will, so new appointments and address book entries can be set up on the PC instead. Plus, if you only need to receive rather than send email while you're travelling, the lack of a touchscreen or proper keyboard may not be a problem.

One other option is a device with a thumb keyboard, such as a RIM BlackBerry or a Palm Treo 600. These make it easy to send email, although the BlackBerry's real advantage is its ability to receive email immediately, whereas most other mobile devices wait for you to tell them to make a connection and download whatever is waiting.

the challenge of wireless security

Companies need to be committed to using all available techniques and devices to prevent their security being compromised, warns Nick Langley, business and technology writer

Peculiar chalk marks are appearing on the walls and pavements of our towns and cities. They bear some resemblance to the symbols once used by tramps to tell each other about softhearted householders and other sources of food and shelter. However, these new symbols alert passers-by to the fact that they are within range of an open wireless network, which they can use to access the Internet from their laptops.

'War chalking', as it's known, uses software that can be downloaded free from the Internet, which detects wireless nodes and identifies whether or not they are open or secure. Most war chalkers, like most hackers, are harmless nuisances, driven by nosiness, or what they regard as an intellectual challenge. They do no damage, but may send an email to show they've been there.

But others have darker motives. "If people are so stupid as to set up their wireless access points so that they are open, then serve them right. The world is full of bad systems administrators who need to be taught a lesson," declares one cyber-guerrilla.

EXECUTIVE SUMMARY

☐ a wireless policy that recognises the importance of security is a must for any company that is using wireless technology. It should be tested and reviewed regularly

☐ protection through certified equipment has had a chequered past. However, new solutions are being developed all the time

☐ one simple solution is to separate the wireless network from the main wired network using a virtual private network (VPN)

The same tools and techniques could also be used by criminals, or by people who trade in commercially sensitive information. There are even reports that 'spam' advertisers have taken advantage of open wireless access points to send out their mass-mailed rubbish, flooding the network and causing possible embarrassment to the company whose Internet connection has been hijacked.

The risk is even more serious if the wireless network is connected to the company's wired network. An open wireless access point could provide a backdoor to data and applications that are otherwise well protected.

monitoring the problem

To get some idea of the scale of the problem, KPMG in London set up a 'honeypot', a dummy wireless access point containing monitoring software, which gathers survey data about wireless hacking as a marketing tool for their security services. It found that most activity takes place while people are driving to and from work; very little at weekends.

And, AT&T Broadband has sent out 'wardrivers' of its own, which can track down open wireless access points and check whether they're being shared, against the terms of its contracts.

When RSA Security carried out a survey in the City of London, it found that of the 500-odd wireless nodes identified, more than one third were not secure. Some had simply kept the 'default' security settings supplied by the vendors. Because vendors want to make the equipment as easy as possible to set up, 'default' usually means that security is turned off. Others had not made use of the security technology supplied. Many networks uncovered by RSA had been given names that identified the company. These names were regularly broadcast as part of the networks' routine operations, telling potential hackers exactly what they had stumbled across.

"A company may not have a wireless strategy, but it's there whether they know about it or not, because it's become so inexpensive for individuals to go down to PC World and buy their own access point and set it up," warns analyst Gartner Group. "Get a wireless network policy set up and enabled."

Today's subscribers will find it much easier than the early adopters to keep wireless networking safe. The first generation of Wi-Fi certified equipment used something called Wired Equivalent Privacy (WEP). But bearing in mind that wired network security has evolved over three decades, and has been tested repeatedly to destruction, it was unlikely that wireless technology developers would get their equivalent right first time round. Sure enough, it soon emerged that WEP had easily exploitable holes in it.

industry compliance

The second attempt was Wi-Fi Protected Access, or WPA. Since September 2003, the Wi-Fi Alliance, the wireless industry association, has required equipment to have WPA before awarding Wi-Fi compliance certification.

As of February 2004, more than 175 products from some 40 manufacturers have received WEP security certification.

The Wi-Fi Alliance warns that since WEP can be compromised, it should not be considered a secure mechanism to protect a wireless network. "We recommend that WEP be dropped in favour of WPA as soon as is feasible," it says.

Anyone who bought their wireless networking equipment before the last quarter of 2003 is likely to have WEP rather than WPA, and it's worth checking even when equipment has been bought more recently.

WPA is frequently described as the state-of-the-art wireless network security technology, but it is still immature, and many technology commentators regard it as another temporary fix on the way to a reliable security standard.

While the industry works on the next generation of wireless security, there are plenty of proven technologies that can be used. One simple way is to set up the wireless network as a sub-network, separated from the main wired network by a firewall. This can be developed into a fully functional virtual private network (VPN). VPN packages are available off-the-shelf. They provide a combination of a firewall, security protocols and encryption that creates a kind of tunnel through the Internet or other public network, between an externally used PC such as a laptop, and the main corporate network (see box below).

But, analyst Bloor Research warns, even when wireless access points are secured by software, a hacker could still 'borrow' an access point and crack it open if the physical security is poor. "Wireless technology, like the Internet, increases the number of connections into a business and magnifies bad practices."

Processor maker Intel points out that the limited distance range of wireless networks can be used as part of the security strategy. Placing wireless access points near the middle of your building, and avoiding outward-facing walls and windows, reduces the vulnerable zone beyond the boundaries of the workplace. Reducing the broadcasting strength of the access point can also help. And it may be better not to provide coverage in some areas. For example, do employees really need wireless access in the car park?

VIRTUAL PRIVATE NETWORKS

Most businesses should use virtual private network (VPN) technology to secure Wi-Fi connections. A VPN works by creating a secure virtual tunnel from the end user's computer through the Internet to a company's servers and networks.

To access a VPN-protected Wi-Fi network, users need special software on their mobile device that encrypts and decrypts data as it is sent and received across the Internet. They also need a password that is authenticated by the VPN software before they are able to connect to the network.

There are many types and levels of VPN technology, costing upwards of £10,000. At the other end of the scale, Microsoft provides a basic, free VPN product for its customers. You can also buy a VPN service from many business Internet service providers and wireless network operators.

SECURITY TIPS

☐ all wireless access points and all network interface cards used in laptops and other computers, should be approved by whoever is responsible for IT security. Draw up a list of approved suppliers, and make it clear that using equipment from any other source will be regarded as a serious breach of discipline

☐ use a virtual private network to protect all network traffic. Set the VPN up so it excludes unauthenticated users, and unencrypted traffic

☐ place wireless access points on separate sub-networks, and put a firewall between the sub-networks and the main corporate network

☐ actively scan for rogue or unknown access points on the corporate network. Use the 'sniffer' and discovery tools the hackers use, such as NetStumbler, or buy a packaged network security solution, or have a security consultant carry out a regular audit

(Sources: Intel, RSA Security, Netgear)

However, we shouldn't be lulled into a false sense of security just because we've kept the network within the corporate boundary. "Wireless passes through air and walls and is not constrained, so just because your antennas don't give it the range of coverage you expect, doesn't mean someone else couldn't tune in from further away," says Bloor Research.

Wireless security requires a combination of old and new technologies, physical security, user education and common sense. Like any security policy, it needs to be regularly tested and reviewed. Possibly the best way of ensuring it is effective is to use the tools available to the network hacking community – and keep up-to-date with the latest versions.

intel
inside

centrino™

MOBILE TECHNOLOGY

TOSHIBA

choosing the right network supplier

Nick Langley, business and technology writer, sets out the issues businesses need to address to secure a suitable network supplier

There are two main reasons for the sudden spread of wireless networking. One is that industry standards are in place, resulting in the availability of mass market products, and the ability to mix and match components from different vendors in the confidence that they will work together.

EXECUTIVE SUMMARY

☐ there's a wide range of suppliers available, but it is generally recommended that businesses match the size of their supplier to the size of their company

☐ if you require a substantial wireless rollout, it is advisable to use more than one supplier so as to spread potential risks

☐ there are advantages to buying now and to waiting. The guiding principle should be: is there a strong business rationale for moving sooner rather than later?

The second is that prices have fallen dramatically. You can now buy a package for a couple of hundred pounds that contains everything you need for a small wireless network in a single box. And setting it up is so easy – you can do it without technical assistance, or even the level of DIY competence needed to assemble your average flat-pack wardrobe.

At the top end of the scale, vendors and analysts are reporting that networks with a couple of hundred users are being built for four-figure sums – in terms of the hardware outlay, at least. This is a fraction of the cost of installing the cabling for a conventional wired network, and can be done in a fraction of the time. Like conventional networks, however, larger wireless networks still need to be carefully planned and managed.

There's no reason not to buy your first wireless network package from the high street for setting up a small pilot system that can provide email and Internet access but is isolated from the company network. However, for more serious use, you will need to find one or more partners who can meet all your needs:

- [ ] designing and installing the network

- [ ] integrating it with the existing wired network

- [ ] supplying and supporting applications

- [ ] helping with problem solving and upgrades

- [ ] training your staff

identifying potential suppliers

There's a wide choice of potential suppliers available, from the big manufacturers such as Cisco and their resellers, telecommunications companies such as BT, consultants and systems integrators, as well as specialists in network products and services of all sizes.

As a rule of thumb, you should match the size of supplier to the size of your own business. Many larger suppliers are developing strategies to capture a share of the SME market, which has been far more buoyant in its IT spending than the corporate market. But a supplier whose processes are geared to governments and multinational corporations may struggle to adapt to the needs of a smaller business. Similarly, while a very small company may offer good terms to win your business, they may struggle to deliver the required level of service and support.

Track record is particularly important. You need to know that the supplier has been successful with other customers. You also need to know that they will be around to support you in years to come since wireless is a relatively new business (although it's been around far longer in the education sector, particularly in schools).

It is worth looking for a company with a record of success in fixed-wire networking, as the likelihood is that you will be integrating wireless with your existing wired network.

WHAT ELSE IS ON OFFER FROM SUPPLIERS?

. The driver for installing a wireless network may well be to save cabling costs in the office, or to add flexibility for staff to work in 'touch down' points. But many firms will also want to rollout mobile applications that can be used remotely, by 'road warriors' and other professionals.

A large range of applications tailored to mobile working are now on offer, both for general purpose systems such as salesforce automation, and for 'vertical' applications specific to certain industries, such as logistics. There is also a growing class of 'middleware' – software that helps to build a bridge between office and mobile environments and also operate across Wi-Fi, mobile phone and private wireless networks.

Another important class of wireless offerings is management and security: apart from the physical components needed to equip a company wireless network, a significant market is now springing up that is addressing the specific concerns of operating wireless networks.

spreading the risk

If you are shopping for a substantial wireless rollout that will, say, involve accessing applications remotely, it is unlikely that you'll find all your requirements in one supplier. As industry analyst Gartner Group says: "In most cases, several partners and suppliers will be necessary for the deployment of wireless technology and services. Through 2005, unstable markets and ongoing consolidation will reduce the number of wireless players. It is very risky to rely on long-term relationships or accept tight links with these players. Wireless initiatives should include careful evaluation of the status of potential partners and suppliers."

(See also box for a brief run-down of other players in the mobile arena likely to be of interest.)

Ask a number of suppliers to visit the office to conduct a site survey, since what works on paper may not work in practice. An onsite inspection will determine the number of base stations you need and identify any troublesome spots where wireless access points won't provide the coverage you expect.

The next step is to get a detailed quote that should include all the associated services, from design and installation, to upgrades and ongoing support. You will probably find that the cost of equipment is a fraction of the overall quote, perhaps as little as ten per cent.

There are lessons to be drawn from the pioneering experience of the education sector. "We asked a number of different suppliers to do site surveys of our school," one headmaster reported. "The results varied dramatically, both in the cost and the number of base stations we needed. Fortunately, two of the suppliers said pretty much the same thing. We went with one of those as they also promised the best after-sales care."

are standards reliable?

Wireless networking has the potential to develop into a commodity market, where products from different vendors have to meet the same set of standards and expectations, and so will vary only slightly on features and price. But it hasn't happened yet.

Potential IT purchasers are frequently advised not to buy early, on the basis that prices invariably come down and problems are ironed out if you wait. However, the trouble is that once you've waited, there's usually something new on the horizon: should you wait again?

forward and backward compatibility

The development of wireless network technology is so fast that customers who decide not to risk the 'bleeding edge' must instead live with the fear that their equipment will quickly become obsolete. Forward and backward compatibility is therefore very important: can your supplier demonstrate that the equipment you buy will not be left up a blind alley when the next generation of faster, more functional and reliable wireless technology becomes available?

Old wireless networking equipment tended to use fixed-function 'innards' which could not adapt when the technology moved on. Newer equipment should have programmable processors, which can adapt.

Certification by industry body the Wi-Fi Alliance should provide a guarantee that the equipment you buy meets current standards, and should be inter-operable with any other certified equipment. The Wi-Fi Alliance claims that wireless networking products that don't go through its certification process

CHOOSING YOUR WIRELESS NETWORK VENDOR

☐ consider the capabilities, capacity and availability of your vendor to work with you throughout the life of your wireless system – from the initial planning, network analysis, design and site survey, through integration and installation of the system, to ongoing service and support

☐ before the initial installation, invest time in the plan and design of your system. While a wireless system will enable worker mobility, the supporting infrastructure is not mobile and its placement for performance and coverage must be carefully planned

☐ assess your requirements and develop a plan for day-to-day management, service, and support to ensure your wireless network investment will continue to meet the changing demands of your business

Source: mobility vendor Symbol Technologies

have 'catastrophic' failure rates. The certification tests are stringent: more than a quarter of candidate products fail the first time round.

buy now or wait?

Gartner Group predicts that wireless networking technology will continue to fall in price during 2004 while, at the same time, becoming more functional and better integrated with other kinds of network and mobile technology. New standards are pending which will enable wireless networks to be better integrated into the wired network infrastructure.

So waiting may have its advantages: you will get more for your money, it will be more reliable, and easier to integrate with your existing IT systems. But in the meantime, you could miss out on competitive advantage.

The bottom line is whether you can see a strong business advantage in moving sooner rather than later. Gartner Group says an effective wireless project should provide a return on investment within 18 months, so it's worth carrying out a cost and benefit study. Significant savings are unlikely to come simply from improved productivity and convenience alone: you should be identifying specific applications, and seeking suppliers who can support them.

If you decide the time's not right, you can still dip a toe in the water by buying a wireless network in a box from a high street retailer.

wi-fi futures

Bryan Betts, business and technology writer, reflects on what companies will be doing with wireless in five years' time – and beyond

Wireless computing frees the user from concerns of geography or location. It means, for example, that sales people can access the latest price list while in a client's office, and that our phones switch from cellular operation outdoors onto the company's wireless network when we walk indoors, even in the middle of a call.

Sitting in a meeting, we'll be able to write notes on the screen of a tablet PC and have these filed instantly to the office network, with automatic conversion of handwriting into text, if desired. As we walk back into the office, the network will detect our presence and fire up a short-range 'Bluetooth' wireless connection to synchronise new messages and appointments onto the smartphones and personal organisers in our pocket.

And, while we're driving, the car's own information system will be downloading urgent messages and reading them to us over the stereo. It will also keep track of any problems developing and book itself in for a service as needed, communicating wirelessly with the garage's diagnostic server via the home broadband.

EXECUTIVE SUMMARY

- [ ] continuing advances in technology means that wireless connectivity will become seamless in terms of usage and billing

- [ ] voice-over-IP will be commonly used and will be compatible with wireless office and home networks

- [ ] flexible working will become even more popular with mobile devices seamlessly interchanging between ethernet and GPRS

Delivery drivers will use wireless too. Bluetooth will connect their handheld computers to the new third generation (3G) mobile phone systems in the cab for job schedules, and a GPS satellite receiver will fix the location and provide mapping. Meanwhile, a wireless printer will output receipts and other documents.

The use of technology will become more natural: we can type, write or speak into our laptops or PDAs as we choose. Wireless will then make those devices appear more intelligent, able to tap into networks for information and extra resources, as needed.

Wireless will also provide alternatives to cables for broadband itself. Within villages, a wireless network allows neighbours to share a single broadband connection, and the WiMax wireless broadband services currently under development will provide much higher capacity over distances of up to 50 kilometres, well beyond the reach of current broadband wireless systems.

making it work

The first requirement is for wireless connectivity to become seamless in terms of usage and billing. Mobile phone network operators believe that they are well placed to take over the public wireless hotspot business on both accounts: once you go out of hotspot range your mobile device will automatically switch over to GPRS or its 3G equivalent, and all of this will be billed to a single account.

Meanwhile, intelligent agents within your company network or the cellular network will monitor your current connection speed, adjusting what gets delivered to avoid overloading the link. For example, if you are on the GPRS mobile phone system then the non-urgent software upgrades or data synchronisation for your PC will be postponed until you are back in range of a Wi-Fi connection in the office or at a hotspot.

For line-of-business applications, wireless handheld devices such as Palms, Pocket PCs and smartphones will allow us to get information when and where we need it. They will still need some local storage, though only for those times and places where a connection is either unavailable or impractical. Applications too will be connection-aware, operating fully on-line when it is possible and cost-effective to do so, adjusting their demands when only a slow connection is available, and otherwise storing transactions off-line for later processing.

Among the organisations working here are Intel, whose Mobilized Software Initiative aims to help software companies develop 'connection-aware' programs, and Citrix, which specialises in remote access to office applications.

Remote access allows a program to run on the office network via the screen and keyboard of a PC elsewhere. It is used for security and because it makes applications easier to manage. It presents particular issues with networking, though, because while it can work well over even quite slow connections, it cannot work at all if there is no link.

voice and data convergence

Voice telephony too is moving to all-digital systems based on the same 'IP' (Internet protocol) networking technology used by office networks and the Internet, and called 'voice-over-IP'. Some cordless phones already use voice-over-IP via wireless company networks, and as this becomes the norm it will be built into mobile phones too.

In fact, in five years' time, voice-over-IP will be the norm for organisations of all sizes and, more importantly, will work with our wireless office and home networks.

By then, office cordless phones will actually be wireless handheld PCs, while audio-equipped personal organisers will not only be able to operate as phones, but they will be able to convert speech to text, and text to speech – tasks which today need much more powerful PCs.

The third generation of mobile phones, 3G, also provides IP data connections at broadband speeds but still uses traditional voice telephony techniques. Subsequent generations (which, given the delays to 3G, will probably not be in place for perhaps 10 years) will use IP for voice as well.

teleworking

Remote working and home working are going to become more popular in the next few years, not least because of legislation promoting flexible working. We may not want to work from home all the time, but when we're there we need to stay in touch and have full access to all our usual network information and other resources.

Offices are expected to have cables slung around them, but relatively few homes are wired up with network cables, even though more and more of us have broadband installed. Its simplicity of installation means that wireless networking will become the normal way to network a home to share that broadband connection.

For those of us who do not live in an area blessed with cable TV coverage or access to ADSL, other forms of wireless networking will come to the rescue (see chapter 7). Community wireless schemes can very cheaply extend the reach of wired broadband by up to a few kilometres, and commercial wireless broadband technologies such as WiMax will take it even further.

Wireless not only makes it easier to work from home, but you can work in other places too, from hotels and coffee shops onwards. Virtual private networks (VPNs) with encryption make sure that the connection is secure, and seamless roaming from Wi-Fi to GPRS will allow our mobile devices to use the best link available at the time.

Roaming between wireless networks will have improved too, so it won't matter that we do not have a subscription to the coffee house's system. Instead, the companies involved will sort that out in the background, probably with our mobile phone company acting as arbitrageur, for a modest fee, of course.

the Internet as a utility

Even better, if there is a community network about, such as Consume.net in the UK or NYCwireless.net in New York City, we can get this connectivity for free.

And not all commercial providers charge for wireless network access, either. However, in such instances, users clearly have little comeback if the wireless connection should turn out to be congested and relatively slow. But, as wireless usage grows there is no immutable law that says it has to remain a paid-for extra, and some businesses have already decided to offer it for no extra charge, as a way of winning custom.

Perhaps they are right, and the availability of wireless Internet access is no different from other things one might expect of a cafe, say, such as electric lights and comfy chairs, and having the tables wiped clean regularly. If so, there are some interesting times ahead, both for the networking industry and for us as users and customers.

hot tips for hotspot users

Bryan Betts provides some practical advice for the wireless traveller

1. get the products: many laptops now have wireless networking built in, or you can easily add a PC Card adapter. Most hotspots support the common wireless networking standard (known as 802.11b), but it can be worth looking for dual or triple-mode adapters which also support 802.11a or 802.11g, as if these are available you will get a faster connection.

2. get the software: the Windows XP system is pretty good at detecting what wireless networks are around and helping you connect to them. Failing that, laptop makers such as Toshiba or IBM often supply their own software to set up your wireless connection.

3. stay secure: on a wireless network you are vulnerable to hackers and eavesdroppers. Put personal firewall software on your laptop – Black Ice and Zone Alarm are good names here – and to connect back to HQ you will need VPN (virtual private network) software set up too. Also, disable file sharing on your computer. It should go without saying that you need up-to-date anti-virus software, and perhaps also encryption software to hide your data in case the laptop gets lost or stolen.

4. find some hotspots: check out your hotel's website to see if it offers wireless networking. There are several directories of public wireless hotspots on the Web, (see Appendix III) so you can look up the airports you'll be using, the conference centre, and even the coffee shops in the vicinity of where you are staying.

5 **sort out the business side:** most public hotspots work on a subscription or daily fee basis. This is pretty simple but subscriptions rarely transfer from one hotspot company to another. An alternative is to use a roaming service such as Gric, iPass or Boingo – in return for a monthly subscription, you can use a range of companies' hotspots, though not all of them, of course.

6 **have a backup plan:** although public wireless hotspots are increasingly common, they are not everywhere. Your hotel may offer wired Ethernet instead, or a data-port for dial-up access, so take a wired network adapter and a modem too. And of course there is GSM/GPRS and now 3G mobile phones, which you can access either by using infrared or Bluetooth to connect your laptop to a mobile phone, or via a card plugged into the laptop.

7 **get connected:** assuming your PC detects the network, and your connection software sorts out the set-up, in most cases you just open a Web browser window and log on, entering your credit card information if you are paying ad hoc or your subscription details if you have signed up for a service. Some roaming services, such as Gric and iPass, have their own software which can handle this for you, so make sure you install it before you go. Lastly, if you are accessing your corporate systems, you will probably need to activate your VPN software to create a secure 'tunnel' back to base.

8 **find a strong signal:** radio waves are blocked or reflected by walls, so it can take some experimentation to figure out where the best reception is. Think too about where the base station might be located – for example, if you can't find a signal in an airport and can't get into the business lounge, try sitting just outside the lounge, as the radio signal will often stretch just far enough.

9 **get busy:** a wireless connection can be used for just about anything you would do on your office network – email, Web browsing, even accessing corporate applications and databases (given the right security, of course). Bear in mind that it will not be as fast as the office network, but if you are used to using a modem on the road, it should be a great improvement.

10 **test it before you go:** find which of your local coffee shops and hotels have hotspots, and try working from a couple of them for a few hours. Nothing beats a real world test, and it's a lot easier when you're yards from technical support rather than thousands of miles away.

a 'day in the life' of a wireless user

David Horwood, Managing Director of ihotdesk, an IT consultancy and outsourcing specialist. See www.ihotdesk.com

05.30 Alarm.

06.00 Synchronise email over home wireless broadband access, so can review messages on Gatwick Express into Victoria.

07.10 On the train using tablet computer, lining up mail responses and new mail for clients and colleagues.

08.00 Arrive at Great Eastern Hotel for breakfast seminar on 'voice over IP' – a new way to talk over the Internet. We like to network and keep abreast of the market.

09.35 Fleeting visit to Starbucks to use the T-mobile hotspot to synchronise email. I don't stop for a latte – they get enough business out of ihotdesk in a day.

10.00 Visiting a potential serviced office at Angel. Kept waiting for 15 minutes, which allows me to check my email on a Handspring Treo smartphone – we use Orange GPRS services on our smartphones and PDAs, configured to work with Microsoft Exchange Server in our data centre. Make notes on the Treo about the office, which will later synchronise with Outlook. I rely totally on 'digital ink' – on the tablet PC or smartphone. I know this sounds sad, but I do have to practice what I preach.

10.40 Short walk down to Barbican to review another potential office. salesperson insists I don't have to type my notes in my smartphone, as she has a weighty sales pack for me with all the info. She doesn't realise the sales pack will go in the bin when I leave or gather dust at home. My electronic notes are always at hand.

12.00 Arrive at a client's office on the Albert Embankment. Kept waiting in reception for 20 minutes, which allows me to respond to my email on the smartphone.

13.00 Lunch with a client and colleague, all calls on divert, and look forward to an interesting lunch. Our client has just returned from two weeks consulting in Baghdad. He's relates his experience with technology out there and we discuss satellite communications I always enjoy my time with this client, straight talking and knows what is important. He insists on paying this time.

15.00 Arrive at the IoD, 123 Pall Mall – key in the 'user-friendly' password (he means it's rather long winded – Ed.) and get Wi-Fi access to our company's accounts system. I need to review how much we have spent with a supplier in the last 12 months.

15.15 Meet with supplier at the IoD who has developed a system to reduce the workload of our server management team. I'm able to agree a reduced charge for new developments, after showing him our last 12 month spend with him. He also uses his Wi-Fi enabled laptop to give me a demo of the new his offering.

16.00 Phone call with journalist (IoD a little noisy this afternoon for telephone conversation).

17.05 At Putney Bridge station on the tube, able to reply to an important email regarding a project that is just going live.

17.15 Arrive at estate agent in Wimbledon. I'm moving closer to London, so I don't have to have too many more 5.30 starts.

Kept waiting for an estate agent, but gives me time to receive email – the good news that the project has been signed off and the client is happy.

18.30 Head back to Gatwick on the train. Reading the Evening Standard because I feel a real twit using a smartphone or the tablet PC on a slow, slam door train. You have to be mindful of security.

19.30 Arrive home - start synchronising mail and a few documents across the Wi-Fi broadband connection. This is my daily backup to our servers. Finish off a proposal to a prospective new client while half-watching Eastenders.

20.45 Our helpdesk escalates a problem to me from one of my clients.

21.00 Chat on-line with one of our database consultants who has responded to the problem – his moniker is 'Leave it to me'.

22.00 'Leave it to me' messages to say, 'All fixed and OK.'

23.00 My wife sets the alarm for 7.30. I can't work the alarm – too technical – but no meeting until 2pm tomorrow, so can work at home first thing.

resources

industry and government

Wi-Fi Alliance – a non-profit international association formed in 1999 to certify interoperability of wireless network products. The site has good content on topics such as security, and also contains a benefits calculator.

www.wi-fi.org

The Institute of Directors, in association with Toshiba, provides the latest information and advice about wireless computing at:

www.iod.com/wirelesscomputing

The Department of Trade and Industry has a wireless technologies pack at:

www.dti.gov.uk/bestpractice

public hotspot providers

Boingo Wireless	www.boingo.com
BT Openzone	www.bt.com/openzone
iPass	www.ipass.com
Swisscom Eurospot	www.swisscom-eurospot.com
Surf and Sip	www.surfandsip.com
T-Mobile	www.t-mobile.co.uk/hotspot
ReadytoSurf	www.readytosurf.co.uk

hotspot finders

www.totalhotspots.com

www.wi-fizone.org

www.myhotspots.co.uk

www.jiwire.com

media and other sources

Palo Wireless	www.palowireless.com
ZD Net UK	www.zdnet.co.uk/specials/wifimap/what.htm
WiFi Networking News	www.wifinetnews.com
Mobileinfo	www.mobileinfo.com
NewsWireless	www.newswireless.net
Cutting the cord: the commercial impact of mobile computing (Nortel/Economist Intelligence Unit)	www.nortelnetworks.com
Unwired newsletter	www.unwired.eu.com
The Complete Guide to Flexible Working	www.flexibility.co.uk/guide
The Excellent Virtual Manager	www.roffeypark.com

user groups

Mobile Computer Users Group	www.mcug.org.uk
Wireless Ecademy	http://wireless.ecademy.com

events

Wi-Fi Planet Conference & Expo (27-29 October 2004 – Novotel London West Hotel & Convention Centre)	www.jupiterevents.com/wifi/london04

glossary

3G
The new generation of mobile phone technology that allows high-speed, always on data communication.

802.11 standard
802.11, or IEEE 802.11, is the radio technology used for wireless local area networks (WLANs) and Wi-Fi hotspots. It comprises several standards operating in different radio frequencies that give various performance options.

Access point
The wireless base station that connects wireless enabled computers and other devices to a wired network.

Bandwidth
The capacity of a network – current wireless systems can provide from 11 megabits per second to 54 megabits a second.

Bluetooth
A short range wireless standard for connecting devices such as headsets and printers to laptop computers and mobile phones.

Broadband
A fast 'always on' Internet connection.

Firewall
A software and/or hardware system that prevents unauthorised traffic into and out from a company network or individual PC.

GPRS
General Packet Radio Services – an interim technology between GSM mobile phones and the new 3G networks, it allows always on, Internet-style data communications.

GSM
Global System for Mobile communication – the widespread conventional mobile phone standard in the UK that will be replaced by GPRS and 3G.

Hotspot
An area where people access a Wi-Fi service, such as a railway station, airport, coffee shop, or any public place such as a public reception area.

PAN
Personal area network – a short range network connecting devices such as headsets and PDAs, usually via Bluetooth .

PDA
Personal digital assistant – a handheld computer with organiser functions.

RFID
Radio frequency identification – a method of remotely storing and retrieving data using tags that can be attached to or built into a product.

Smartphone
A mobile phone/PDA combination, allowing voice, Internet access and organiser functions.

Site survey
Surveying an office or other location for the best provision of wireless coverage.

VoIP
Voice over IP (Internet Protocol) – a way of transmitting voice communications on the Internet, both within and outside a company.

VPN
Virtual private network – a way of providing a secure, private 'tunnel' through the Internet to allow staff to access office computers.

Wi-Fi
Wireless fidelity – refers to wireless communications based on the 802.11 standard.

Wireless adapter
A device such as card that slots into a computer to allow wireless connectivity.

WLAN
Wireless local area network.

Sponsor a Director's Guide

with more than **60 titles** produced, the **Director's Guide** series is a **highly successful** business publishing venture

Each guide is produced in conjunction with a major blue-chip sponsor – from Oracle and Grant Thornton to Toshiba and Fedex – and each is sent free over 53,000 individual members of the IoD in the UK.

Director's Guides cover a diverse range of topics – from e-commerce to growth finance, from customer care to management buy-outs. Research shows the series forms a key part of IoD members' business reading, with a high retention value and pass-on readership. The direct benefits to the sponsor include:

☐ 53,000 individual director-level circulation

☐ strong position as an authority in its specialist area

☐ authorship of up to three chapters

☐ full co-branding with the IoD

☐ seven pages of exclusive colour advertising, including two positions on the covers

☐ a reply-paid card bound into the guide, for direct response

☐ 3,000 sponsor copies

☐ broad press coverage

For further enquiries, please contact Business Development and Sponsorship on: **020 7766 8555** or e-mail us at: busdev@iod.co.uk